# RV Quick Start Guide:

## An Alternative Lifestyle for Today's Economy

**Janet Smith**

ISBN-13:
978-1502538055

ISBN-10:
1502538059

In the Beginning...5
Costs... 7
Online Income... 8
Staying Connected Online... 14
"Real Life" Income
What Type of RV is Right for YOU?... 19
Determining Your Lifestyle and Comfort Levels... 29
Where to Park It?... 32
Basic Maintenance... 40
Weight Distribution... 50
Packing Your Stuff for Moving... 53
Personal Safety... 56
Where Are You From?... 58
Driving, and Planning Your Routes... 58
Towing... 60
Off Into the Sunset... 62

## In the Beginning...

I'm writing this to give you both inspiration, and a reality check. I've been living this RV lifestyle for a few years now, and it's a good life. I planned for it, and I hope to help you plan for it too, not only in the nuts and bolts sense, but mentally and emotionally.

You may have hit upon hard times, are struggling to make ends meet, and think selling the house and hitting the road may be the way to go. Or maybe, you are distressed by current politics, and feel the need to prep and bug out. Perhaps you sense the End Times coming. Or maybe you are the adventurous and artistic type, who wants to experiment with off the grid, green living. Or maybe a combination of all of the above (or none of the above). Whatever your reasons, you are not exactly in step with what other people expect from life. You want less, yet expect *more*... LIFE!

I'll begin with my own story, it's the one I know best, and perhaps we'll find some common ground. I, like most people, thought I would grow up, get married, have some kids, the house with a picket fence... then times changed, and I thought, I'll have a career as an artist... what really wound up happening was, I found myself in a dead end social services job, surrounded by people who were crippled by fear and stagnation. Not only the mentally disabled and ill it was my job to "rehabilitate", but my coworkers, and the system itself. I was caught in some sort of a web, on a treadmill, the same thing, over and over, and no one else seemed to notice. Everyone around me seemed crippled by fear of change, uncomfortably content in their own stagnation, slowly turning into cartoon characters of who they really should have been. And worse, the whole narrow "system" was boxing me into the same fate.

I was trapped, in a low income, dead end job. All I could afford was low income housing. I was constantly surrounded by people riddled with fear, stagnation, and sickness, desperately trying to escape their condition through drugs, alcohol, promiscuity... *that was not me!* I had nothing to lose; "normal life" had not given me the family, the friends, the home, the career that should have been. It was time for me to take matters into my own hands, get creative, get bold, start building a different sort of life, with different rules and expectations. It took years (and years!) but I taught myself the skills necessary to build an online business. I didn't go out, I didn't party, I planned, and I built. The only "escapism" I had was watching the Travel Channel; I never had the money, or time, to travel. All I did was work (50-80 hours a week) to pay bills. I didn't have a family to visit, only the people on the job. I wanted to see more of the world, and of life, before I died. And that's where the plan to escape in an RV was born.

Can you relate to any of that? I'll bet you can.

There are no guarantees in life, but you can hedge the odds with planning, and a serious dose of personal truth and honesty; if you think you will score a really cheap RV off Craigslist, then "live for free at Walmart", you may have a serious reality check in your future. Nothing worthwhile in life comes cheap, or is it free. That's not to say you can't score a great deal, or supplement your camping fees with boondocking, or even live fulltime urban stealth camping. But there will be trade offs. And expenses!

*Where to Begin?*

*First, before you move into your RV, have a big yard sale, or go to the flea market, and get rid of anything you don't really need! Then, get rid of even more stuff by donating it to charity.* Then, there are three main things you need to think about, and plan around; your income, the type of RV best suited to you, and where you are going to park it.

## Costs

Everyone wants to know, "How much does it cost?" They want to see a detailed chart, breaking down every little expense, as if every RVer is living the same life, and as if food and gas prices aren't ever increasing. *So, I'm not doing a break down chart!* If you have credit card debt, that will remain the same. You will still spend the same amount on food. If you financed your RV, you can count that as rent or a mortgage, as well as any camping fees you might incur. But, even with an RV payment, and paying for a space, you will most likely come out cheaper than rent or a mortgage, and your utilities bills will either be gone, or, if where you are parked charges for electric, much, much less, even with buying propane. So you might figure, overall, the cost may be a few hundred to a thousand dollars less, depending on how much you were paying before to live in a house or apartment, and how much you are paying now for your RV, and a place to park it. And, are you parking it in an RV park in California, or boondocking on BLM land in Arizona? And how much does gas cost? Good question, ask that next year, and the answer will be "more". Are you driving across country constantly, putting in 1,000 miles a month, or sitting parked for a month at a time? Are you driving a Class B that gets 15 mpg, or a Class A that gets 8 mpg? How much does it cost is something you will have to figure out yourself, according to your own situation.

## Online Income

Of course, many people may be planning to keep the job they have, or continue with their schooling; they just can't afford to keep up with all the bills and rent anymore, and think living in an RV might be the answer to reducing costs. It might be, but finding ways to make money on the side never hurts, and might actually help you situation.

I chose to build an online business, using the psychological knowledge I had gained working in social services. Many would-be fulltime RV escapees feel that an online income is ideal, and in many ways, it is. But there is no "magic get rich quick formula" to succeeding. You need to be honest with yourself; are you willing to learn basic HTML and how to set up and maintain a blog? Are you willing to learn the principles of SEO (search engine optimization)? Are you willing to study the psychological principles of marketing? And most importantly, do you have an area of expertise or interest, that you can use to dominate your niche market? Be willing, and prepared, to spend a lot of time on your learning curve, and thanks to Google and the other search engines, that learning curve, when it comes to SEO and internet marketing, is always moving!

I'll help you out with this a little bit right now; all I can do is throw out some leads, but you need to really pursue this on your own, do some googling and participate in some forums. Your friends can help out, but no one can build your business, or more importantly, maintain it, for you.

***OK, let's get started with the online business!***

First thing you need to figure out is, your niche market. It could be almost anything, but preferably something you are knowledgeable about, have a passion for, and that other people are interested in. It could be a craft skill you have, music, art, it could be consulting or counseling skills, computer programming, website skills, or marketing skills. Basically, it will break down to selling products and services; yours, other people's, and a combination of both.

## *What are the three key things to consider when pursuing a niche market?*

*Find ways to meet the unique needs of your potential buyers.* What is important to them, what can improve their lives, and the way they do things? For instance, you may have experience as a dog trainer; writing ebooks and creating online training seminars that are breed specific would be a niche. A Pitbull will have different training requirements than, let's say, a Bloodhound. Using this as an example, you would join some breed specific online forums, to find out what was important to those particular breed pet-parents. In addition to your own knowledge, you would study what other expert dog trainers had to say about each breed type. Then you would write your ebooks, and create your websites.

*Learn to speak the language of your niche market.* There are certain key words and phrases unique to each market, as well as different emotional needs and expectations. Using the dog training example again, the Pitbull owner has a different reason for choosing that breed than the Bloodhound owner, and each has a unique language when discussing their breed. In order to convey your expertise, and your products, it's vital to learn the lingo.

*Do some test marketing.* You can do this by investigating your competition online. You can search Amazon, and other online markets, and take a look at the popularity of titles related to your subject. How are they selling? *(Or not selling?)* Study the keywords they are using, the marketing tactics, their prices. And be honest with yourself... is this a market you can relatively easily get a foot hold in?

*Choose an online marketing method and business model*

If you have a talent for writing, and some expertise on a subject, then writing and consulting can be for you. If you don't, you can still make money online with affiliate marketing, and possibly selling on eBay, Etsy, Fiverr, and other auction and sales websites. (Keep in mind, if you are selling real, tangible goods, they need to be small and light! You do live in an RV, with limited storage!)

*What is Affiliate marketing?*

Essentially, it is selling other people's products, for a commission. There are many ways to use affiliate marketing, as an additional sales venue for your niche market (using the dog training example, you could put affiliate links to products such as training collars and books). Affiliate marketers also have blogs and websites devoted to product reviews, use PPC (pay per click advertising on Google, Yahoo and other search engines) to gain a spot at the top of search results, and many other methods. Personally, IMHO, paying for PPC ads hardly ever pays off, unless the items you are trying to sell have a very good profit margin. There are tons of schemes disreputable online marketers use, such as setting up a website and hosting Google AdWords (or some other PPC ad platform) and paying poor people in Third World countries pennies to click on the ads; you see, the websites that host Google AdWords get a small amount for every ad they host which gets clicked. The result for the hapless advertisers is, they spend lots of money for lots of clicks that were absolutely worthless.

*Another way to make money, photography, art and music*

If you are living in an RV, you have to think about art in the context of what can you do on your computer. In this day and age of digital photography and videography, you could also do wedding and special event photography. Also, what kind of photographs and video clips sell to other people selling stuff on the web; there is a market for royalty free images to use on websites, book and CD covers, tee shirts, royalty free video clips, royalty free music for TV commercials, video productions, and more. You can have a lot of creative and artistic license, just about anything you can imagine will have a place. The thing is, your profit margin on each sale will be quite small, so be prepared to produce a lot of work, like hundreds of clips. And you need a good camera, with high definition. If you are traveling in your RV, you can plan trips around scenic areas, and you may even be able to take your travel expenses as a business expense! There are quite a few websites already established where you can sell your royalty free work, just web search "royalty free images" "royalty free music" "royalty free video" to find some. It should be free to join and start selling, *but read the user agreements, to see if any site wants exclusivity; be sure it is OK to sell your work elsewhere, and be sure not to give your copyrights away!* It is best to put your work out on as many platforms as possible, meaning, sell your photos and video clips on as many websites as you can manage, 5, 10, 20!

## *Tee Shirts and Other Swag*

If you have some artistic talent, and a keen sense of what is happening now, you can make a little extra cash online with print on demand tee shirts, coffee mugs, refrigerator magnets and the like. Political and contemporary entertainment satire, jumping on the latest scandals and controversies can be hot sellers. Just be very, very careful not to infringe on any copyrighted material or logos, or say anything that could be construed as threatening to life, defamatory or libel. Two very popular sites to launch such swag are ***cafepress.com*** *and **zazzle.com***. Of course, in order to sell this stuff, you will need to get onto the social networks, stuff some keywords into your titles for the search engines, and maybe do an online press release. Nothing sells itself, marketing!

## *Self Publishing*

There are a few different platforms to self publish your writing, without giving away your copyrights. The best genres for writing are non-fiction, how-to type books, but other genres can also be lucrative, it just depends on your talent, and your marketing ability. In addition to having some skill and talent as a writer, you need to have some basic word processing skills, and the ability to format the book the way the online self publishing platform requires; for a paperback or hard cover, that's usually a PDF document, formatted to the trim size of the book. For ebooks, it could be several different types of formats. (You can often find someone on the Fiverr.com website willing to format it for you for just $5). You may also want to hone your Photoshop skills, to create your own book covers. (Once again, you may find someone to do that for you on Fiverr.com, or some other website). *Two popular online self publishing websites are* **Lulu.com** *and* **CreateSpace.com**, *as well as* **Xlibris.com** *and* **iUniverse.com**. *Amazon Kindle is also a very powerful and popular sales platform for you book.*

Another way to make money writing is to write articles for others. Blog owners are constantly looking for "fresh content" to post on their sites. The optimum length of a blog article is around 400 words. *There are a lot of websites for freelance writers, such as* **Scripted.com, Elance.com, Odesk.com, Writeraccess.com**, *and more, just search "hire freelance writer" to find some, and sign up!*One very important note, if you are writing blog articles for yourself or for others, it is vital you learn the principles of SEO (search engine optimization) and the current levels of optimum keyword density. Getting ranked on the search engines is the whole point of having a website, especially one that is intended to make money.

## Consulting

If you have expertise and authority in a field, such as counseling, car mechanic, advice nursing, computer trouble shooting, tarot reading, or anything else, there are also online platforms for pay-per-minute phone lines, web chat and video chat. These sites are generally free to get started, and collect a percentage of what you charge. Sites like ***Keen.com, LivePerson.com, JustAnswer.com*** are popular, but there are others.

## Computer Related Jobs

You can also work as a freelance computer expert; any and all aspects of website design, script writing, mobile developers, programming, SEO, marketing, these skills are in high demand. You can find freelance work on websites like ***Freelancer.com, Guru.com, Elance.com, Odesk.com*** and others. These sites are international, you will not only be able to find work "virtually" all over the world, but you will also be competing with other freelancers from all over the world, many of whom will work for a fraction of what Americans will. Make your online resume and thumbnail picture exceptional, and your rates competitive.

## Delivering RVs

How do you think RVs get to the dealerships? Someone drives them there. You wouldn't really be able to live fulltime in these RVs, you would need to travel light, and drive straight through, but it is one way to see the country, and live on the road.

## Combine different online money making platforms

There are many different venues with which to market your products and services online. Using the dog training business as an example, you can write and self publish an ebook and a paperback on your particular niche, and get those up on Amazon. You could also self produce a video, on DVD. You will also launch an informative and attractive blog, incorporating the principles of successful, search engine friendly SEO, with direct links to purchase your book, your DVD, as well as some affiliate links to buy other related products, such as a dog training supplies and books. You can also set up an online chat, Skype or a phone line, to give individual training sessions, for a pay per minute fee. Once you start making contacts and creating networks online, you could schedule some in person training seminars in different locations, and use that to map out your trips, and use your traveling expenses as a business expense. Don't forget to make videos for You Tube, Vimeo and other online video sites, to create an audience for your products and services, and drive traffic to your site. That is just the beginning...

## Staying Connected Online

If you are traveling, and especially, if you like to go deep off the beaten path into the wilderness, you won't have an internet connection. Simple fact. You won't. *Most fulltime RVers go with Verizon, because they have the widest coverage, and the strongest signals, but check your area coverage maps. Also, many fulltime RVers use a provider like **Millenicom.com**; they buy bulk GBs in bundles, so you can get more GBs per month for less money, without a contract.* That is another thing to consider; certain activities online can burn up the GBs faster than others... streaming video, online chat, and Skype will put you close to the edge of your plan faster than anything. Uploading a lot of audio and video will also burn up the GBs. So be aware, and keep track of what you need to do when, the coverage maps, and your limits on data. Of course, you can supplement some of your online activity, and make your data plan go further, by using public WiFi connections, like at Starbuck's or McDonald's, or at the campground. It is a good idea, to use, or subscribe to, a "VPN Tunnel". VPN stands for, virtual private network, and it will encrypt your activity when on public networks. The Firefox browser has VPN plug ins available, and you can also subscribe to VPN services.

### Wifi Boosters

You can also get a cellphone signal booster, designed for a car or truck, which can bring up the number of bars you have, either on your phone, or your internet wifi device. This will have an exterior antennae to put on your roof, as well as an interior antennae, on top of which you will ay your device. These can be pricey, but also can be well worth it in staying connected!

*But what about satellite internet?* A lot of people think the logical solution to the internet problem is to get satellite internet; unfortunately, at this time, that is not as practical as it sounds. Satellite internet is actually slower than 3G/4G, and you will need to spend quite a bit of money for the equipment (new, at least $1,500) and it can take up a lot of room, like an entire shelf in a cabinet. Most satellite internet providers are geared to stationary set ups, and will charge a lot for mobile applications. It is absolutely do-able, but if you are looking to live in an RV in order to live more affordably, satellite internet may not be the answer.

## "Real Life" Income

There are quite a few "real life" ways to make money, while living in an RV (or anywhere). Once again, you need to pursue these goals with creativity, focus and determination.

### *Workamping*

You may have heard of "workamping" (work camping). This is an opportunity to work at a camp ground, in exchange for a space, and usually, a small wage. Often, workamping gigs prefer couples; they get two for one that way. And, this is one form of employment where the older RVer and couples may have an advantage over the younger fulltimer and the solo. These jobs often do not pay enough cash to actually live on, (even though you get the free space) and were created with a retiree in mind, someone with a pension or social security check to cover most of their food and personal items. But if you don't have a lot of bills, and can live simply, a younger fulltimer is definitely in the running, especially for the jobs which might be more physical, such as landscaping, clearing brush and construction. You can find workamping opportunities all over; at private camp grounds, as well as state and national parks. There are many forums and websites devoted to workamping, and web searching "workamping" is the best place to start, if this interests you. There are also magazines, such as *Workamper News*, which also has the website, ***workamper.com***.

### *Working at Amazon*

A workamping gig for a younger, single person might be working for Amazon; bet you didn't know, that Amazon hires RVers to pick and pack at their warehouses, during the Christmas buying season! I say this is well suited to a younger person because, the work at Amazon requires long hours, and a certain level of health and physical fitness. If you are disabled or elderly, this is **not** for you!

The "Amazon Camper Force" typically will work 10 hours a day, four days a week, and this involves standing for long hours at a packing station, or running around the warehouse (at least 5 miles per day) picking items, packing boxes, gift wrapping, and other warehouse shipping work. *It is physical work.* Amazon will rent out an entire RV park for their workers, so you get your space for free too. They have locations in Coffeyville Kansas, Fernley

Nevada and Campbellsville Kentucky. Amazon has a good reputation for treating their work force fairly and well, with better than average pay, and they work to to make being a part of the Camper Force rewarding and fun.

## *Temp Agencies*

If you are planning on visiting certain cities and urban areas for a while, you might consider signing up with the local temp agencies. You will need to have a local address (the RV park) and fill out an application and have an interview, to determine what type of work you are suited for. Once you do get a job or two, and get some good feedback, you might be able to transfer your application information to the affiliated temp agency in the next town on your itinerary.

## *Agricultural Jobs*

This includes working on farms and ranches, game reserves, landscaping, but also, working the rodeo circuit, state fairs and Christmas tree sales. Check the workamper websites and magazines for leads.

## *Property Caretaking Jobs*

Property caretaking jobs are definitely available, with resorts and retreats, ranches, house sitting for the wealthy, and more. You can explore caretaking jobs through magazines such as The Caretaker's Gazette, (*website at **caretaker.org***) Also web search "property caretaker jobs" for more websites and forums that may generate leads.

Property caretaking could also include a "night security" gig. You might find a local business, RV or car sales lot, or a construction site that would be willing to let you park at night, in exchange for keeping an eye on things, and calling the police if necessary.

These situations are generally informal, "off the books" unpaid arrangements, a simple exchange for a place to park at night.

***Flea Markets, Art Fairs, Renaissance Faires, Farmer's Markets and Special Events***

Selling on the weekends can be absolutely ideal for a fulltime RVer. Many flea markets, fairs and special events will allow the vendors to park their rig for free, or a nominal fee, during the event. In addition to selling, there are other opportunities, such as collecting gate fees, cleaning up, performing arts, and more, so this could be an ideal opportunity for an artist, actor, musician or psychic reader. Keep in mind, you may need to sell small, light weight items, as storage in an RV is limited. You will need tables, a chair, and an awning, which will need to find space, or you may have to tow a small moving trailer behind your Class A, B or C RV. Clark's Flea Market Guide has up to date listings of flea markets around the country.
*www.theoriginalclarksfleamarketusa.com*

***Where do you find wholesale goods to sell?***

One fast place to start is eBay; search "wholesale lots" and "wholesale lots free shipping". Also, web search "wholesale lots" "flea market". You will find many websites selling wholesale lots, which might involve pallets of returned store merchandise, overstocks, or new stuff from China. If you have a homebase city where you can rent a storage unit, then buying pallets and truckloads might be the way to go. But if you don't, then buying smaller quantities of smaller, light weight items, such as jewelry and DVDs, might be necessary. Also consider the shipping; you will need to stay put, perhaps for a month, waiting on new shipments of sales stock. Shipping can be very costly, so avoid having the items shipped once to your mail forwarding address, then again to your current location.

Make sure you have plenty of change, ones and five dollar bills! Another advantage to flea markets, festivals and fairs, is that it is mostly a cash business, no need for credit cards, Pay Pal, direct deposits, or pay checks. Your customers will simply be handing over cash!

***Don't put all your eggs in one basket...***

Unless you have a pension, or a really secure, well paying job you can take with you, a combination of different money making strategies might be a good idea; an online business, combined with workamping or caretaking, flea marketing and festivals combined with temp agencies, so on and so forth, might be the best bet to keep the RV rolling, with gas money and places to park. The economy can change quickly these days, be prepared to move and change with it!

## What Type of RV is Right for YOU?

There are two types of RVs, towables (trailers) and motorhomes, and there are several classes within these two general classifications. Which one is right for you? That depends on your what type of lifestyle you want to achieve, how much money and what type of resources you have to work with, and what's available on the market.

If you plan on workamping and living in campgrounds, a towable might be the right choice; you will be stationary for perhaps months at a time, and can use your truck to get around and run errands. But if your plan is to move around the country frequently, then a motorhome might be the right choice.

A motorhome is a motor vehicle chassis and living space all in one. This is what most people think of when they hear "RV". There are three types, or classes of motorhome:

**The Class A Motorhome** (and I will also include bus conversions here).

This is the type of RV that looks like a bus. Class A's can be fueled by either gas or diesel. A gas fueled RV will generally be less expensive to buy and maintain, but a diesel RV will have more torque for climbing hills, better braking and suspension and can carry and tow more weight. The "diesel pusher" is a very desirable model, which will hold it's value better than any other. The diesel pusher is so called because the diesel engine is in the back, giving it extra power and fuel efficiency. The Class A can range in length from 26' to 45'.

Ironically, while the Class A is often the most expensive to buy new, you can often find very good deals on used ones; a 10 year old Class A, that was originally a mid-priced model, may go for significantly less than a comparable Class B or C.
That is because they are usually bigger, can't go very far off road, can't be as easily used for urban stealth camping, and have very poor gas mileage. The Class A RV generally has a low bottom clearance, so it does not do well on bumpy dirt roads, and it doesn't take hills all that well. You can't just park it anywhere, you'll be taking up 2-3 spaces in any parking lot, and you simply won't be able to maneuver in certain places.

Of course, there are advantages to the Class A, including the fact that there seem to be quite a few older ones out there with an affordable price tag. Also, they have more space inside, more storage capacity, and are designed for comfortable living. They come with built in generators, large tanks, nice cabinets, queen size beds, as well as fold out sofas, reclining chairs, and dinettes. A Class A would be a good choice for an older person, who needs accessibility, or a couple or a family with kids. They are also good for those who are running a small business on the road, due to their roominess, comfort and storage capacity.

**The Class B Motorhome** (and van conversions)

This is the type of RV that looks like a van, with a higher roof. There are both gas and diesel, and they range in length from 16' to 21'. These days, it seems the Class B is often the priciest used RV; that's because their small size, maneuverability, van like appearance and fair gas mileage makes them today's top choice for urban stealth camping and boondocking. You could live in the city in a Class B, and find parking at night on a quiet side street, industrial area or in a friend's driveway. You can also go across country, with fairly decent gas mileage, and boondock and stealth camp along the way.

The big downside to a Class B is the same as it's biggest advantage; it's small size. Don't underestimate how small it is to live in one of these! Some Class B's have bathrooms, and some don't. The ones that do generally have a sort of all in one plastic closet, with the toilet and shower as one unit. They have small fresh, grey and black tanks, making frequent dumping and filling necessary. There really isn't much outside storage, like in a Class A or C, and very minimal inside storage; if you are OK with having, let's say, three tee shirts, two pairs of pants, two pairs of shorts, one or two sweaters, a pair of boots and a pair of sandals, maybe a jacket plus some underwear, you are good to go. But, if you require a more extensive wardrobe, a library of books, or a lot of tools for your work, rethink the Class B. Also, the kitchens are very small; generally a two burner stove, and a mini fridge, with a tiny sink. If you love gourmet cooking, once again, a Class B might not be for you. But, if you are the adventurous type who likes to travel light, and have a real need to boondock and especially, urban stealth camp, the Class B might be your ticket to freedom.

**The Class C Motorhome**

This is the type of motorhome that looks like a giant camper turtle shell was placed over a big van. Similar in size to Class A, but it has a sleeping space over the cab and are often available in smaller sizes,
lengths from 20' to 32'. Like the Class B, a used Class C motorhome may sell for more than a comparable Class A, for many of the same reasons. The smaller Class C's are (a little) more maneuverable and parkable than a Class A, and the small ones might get away with urban stealth camping. The Class C can

travel most roads, and has a much storage room and amenities as a comparably sized Class A. This may be the way to go if you have children, kids love the overhead beds! If you are a solo or a couple, you could use either the overhead bed, or the regular bed, and convert the other bed to extra storage. This may be a good choice if you plan to make some extra money at flea markets and fairs.

**Truck Campers**

The advantages of a truck camper are many; you can put it on a 4X4 truck, and go deep off road. They are easy to park, and get decent gas mileage. You can keep your camper (and any modifications you made) and put it on a different truck, rather than having to sell the whole thing. The disadvantages are like those of a Class B; may or may not have a bathroom, and if it does, it's very small and minimal. Minimal kitchen, and a minimal amount of storage (although some of the newer truck campers feature slide outs, to make more room). They also have small fresh, grey and black tanks, making frequent dumping and filling necessary. On top of that, you need to exit the camper, in order to gain access to the truck, and drive away; not a good thing in an emergency situation, such as, you are boondocking or stealth camping, and you find yourself under attack by a crazed meth addict, or a highway bandit! Surprisingly, a new truck camper will cost you as much, or even more, than a much larger and better equipt travel trailer, and you might be surprised at the cost of a used truck camper, although there are some very good deals to be had for these versatile units.

## Towable RVs (trailers)

We all know what a trailer is, and there are advantages to towing rather than driving. If you are workamping, staying in places for weeks or months at a time, or just need to reduce your rent, a trailer could be a good choice. Depending on the size of your trailer, you will need a truck, SUV, or van, equipt to tow, which you can use to drive around on an everyday basis. Except for the very smallest travel trailers, a 3/4 ton tow vehicle is the norm, you may even need a one ton truck for the largest 5th wheels and travel trailers. ***And make sure your truck has a tow package.*** *A tow package* is more than just a hitch receptacle; a truck, van or SUV with a factory installed tow package will also have an upgraded transmission, brakes, suspension and drive train, designed for hauling, and the wiring for the towable's brake lights. It is vital that you check your tow vehicle's towing capacity, and make sure it matches your towable! *Unless you custom build your own very small, off road ready unit, towables are not the choice if your goal is deep, off road boondocking, or urban stealth camping.*

I'll break down the different types of towables. There are three main types:

## The Fifth Wheel Trailer

This is the type of trailer that has the extension that goes over the bed of the pick up truck. This is because this type of trailer has a particular type of hitch, similar to those used on a big rig truck, that sits in the bed of the pick up. This type of  hitch, and the fact that the trailer sits over the truck, almost like one unit, makes for easier towing and maneuvering. Also, this extension gives the 5th wheel trailer a two level floor plan, with the bedroom on top, and higher ceilings than any other type of RV. (If you are very tall, this might be the RV for you.) 5th Wheels have plenty of storage, inside and out, full size kitchens, full size bathrooms (some have two bathrooms) and make a great, fulltime home for families with children. They range in size from 20' to 40', but the larger 5th wheels seem more common. There are some older and smaller 5th wheels (like 18'-22', from the 80s and 90s) that can be had for cheap and restored, that could be pulled by a smaller pick up. The disadvatanges of the 5th wheel is it's size and height; you really need to watch the overhead clearance, and you may not fit into many campsites. Also, your full size truck bed will be filled with the 5th wheel hitch, leaving very little room for anything else, and you can't put a shell on it. But that 5th wheel hitch also makes you much less susceptible to jack knifing and fish tailing, thus, it is a safer and more stable tow than a travel trailer.

**The Travel Trailer**

Typically smaller and lighter than a 5th wheel, the travel trailer has a single level floor plan. There are several types of travel trailers. Starting with the smallest:

**The Teardrop** has no bathroom, no tanks, or very small tanks, and just enough room to sleep two people. The kitchen is actually outside; there is a hatch that opens up, with a cook stove and some storage, but no refrigerator,
and maybe a dishpan for a sink. The new, modern Teardrops, such as a T@b brand trailer, often do have an inside, micro-mini kitchen, and may have a micro-mini bathroom, placed at the expense of any storage that might be had. The advantage to a

Teardrop is nearly any fullsized (or even small sized) car can pull it. These are not suited for fulltime living, unless you are really OK with always using the campground bathroom facilities, or, you have a place to park it, such as in the backyard of family or friends, and you can use their bathroom and kitchen.

**The Travel Trailer**, which can range in length from 15' to 35', has all the amenities you will need; depending on the size of the trailer, you will have a full sized (or nearly full sized) bathroom, a full sized kitchen (though counter space may be limited) sofa, dinette, and bedroom (although in the smallest travel trailers, the bed may be in the same room as everything else, with no separating wall).

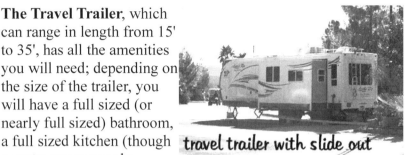
travel trailer with slide out

A third type of travel trailer is the **Toy Hauler**; these are recognized by the fact that the entire back wall is one big door, which folds down as a ramp. They are designed to haul along your ATV, motorcycles, and other "toys". They generally have a bed (for the kids) which will come down from the ceiling in the garage area, and another bedroom towards the front. Despite their rough and tumble origins, many Toy Haulers are quite luxurious inside, with full amenities. A Toy Hauler is a great choice if you like to travel and stay in areas for a week or more at a time, and want a base camp while you explore on your ATV or motorcycle. This could also be a very good choice for someone who is traveling with sales goods for flea markets and art fairs, as the garage area

toy hauler

26

can also be used for storage. *Toy haulers can be either a 5<sup>th</sup> wheel, or a travel trailer.*

The last type of towable I will cover is the **Folding Camping Trailer**. Like the Teardrop, these are very small, and as the name indicates, they fold up (and down) meaning you will need to fold and unfold every time you stop and need to set up. Like the Teardrop, they also generally don't have bathrooms, and minimal kitchens. Also, they have tent canvas siding, so they are not suitable for colder climates. One advantage, they are light weight, can be towed by a large car or small truck, and can go deeper off road than most trailers. But overall, the Folding Tent Trailer is the least suitable for fulltime living.

A Travel Trailer is a nice choice for a solo person, a couple, or a small family, depending on the size of the trailer. ***Once again, you will need a good tow vehicle, preferably a 3/4 to one ton ton truck or SUV*** (except for the smallest trailers) with a tow package, and a truck, van or SUV with a factory installed tow package will have an upgraded transmission, brakes, suspension and drive train, designed for hauling, and the wiring for the towable's brake lights. It is vital that you check your tow vehicle's towing capacity, and make sure it matches your towable! Many people will first buy the towable they want, then buy the truck to match the trailer's weight. Of course, if you already have a tow vehicle with a tow package, find a towable that will match your truck, as far as weight and your truck's towing capacity.

Another thing to be aware of with towables; the manufacturers usually put really poor "trailer quality" tires on them, which are prone to developing bulges and bubbles on the side, and bursting. *A blown tire on a trailer, while it is being towed, can be a very dangerous thing! The trailer can easily begin to fish tail, and cause you to lose control, causing a very serious accident.* Check the carrying capacity of your towable, never overload it, and put car quality tires on it!

## Motorhomes vs. Towables

The type of RV you choose is a personal preference, dependent on your needs and your goals, but there are some basic differences that can help you decide.

### The Pros of a Motorhome

Except for the truck camper, you do not need to leave the motorhome to start your engine.
You don't have to worry about hitching a trailer by yourself.
You are not going to fish tail or jack knife like a trailer might.
It's easier to set up, no hitching and unhitching.
Many motorhomes have self leveling jacks, so there is no need to place blocks or levelers under the wheels.
You can tow a small, economical car, or have a bike or motorcycle on the back.

### The Cons of a Motorhome

If it winds up in the shop, you may need to find somewhere else to live. (Although many RV shops will allow you to "boondock"). Motorhomes tend to be more expensive, even when factoring in a tow vehicle for the towable.
Motorhomes generally have less living space than an equivalent length towable.
Motorhomes depreciate faster.
When towing a car, you cannot back up (you may wreck the car's transmission), you have the cost and maintenance of two vehicles, and you have to hitch, tow, and worry more.

### The Pros of a Towable

They are less expensive and hold their value longer.
They have more living space than a similar sized motorhome.

You can leave the towable at the campsite, and take the tow vehicle on errands.
If your tow vehicle is in the shop, you can still live in the towable.

**The Cons of A Towable**

Towing and hitching/unhitching towables can be a headache.
For the longer towables, parking and finding campsites can be a problem.
Tow vehicles, like 3/4 ton and one ton trucks, can be really expensive, even used.
The gas mileage on a large truck, towing a trailer will be no better than a motorhome, and without towing, your gas mileage will still be bad.
Towables can jack knife or fish tail, causing very serious accidents.

# Determining Your Lifestyle and Comfort Levels

You may have been watching some of the young, hip, urban stealth campers on You Tube, living free on the streets of big, expensive cities in a Class B, while they pursue school, or some cool, hip career. They make it look so easy! So glamorous! So anti-social in a really cool way! Maybe, but hold up, reality check.... Knock, knock, knock, the glare of a flashlight... it's the cops! "You can't park here. License and registration..." Maybe this time, you get off without a ticket, or maybe not. Bang, bang bang! "Gimme all you got!" Oh no! It's a meth addicted gang banger with a mental illness, brandishing a weapon! What do you do? It can, and does happen. You really have to think about this. You really have to look at your environment, and map out the safest, most low profile places you can find, areas where *no one* goes at night. If you are urban stealth camping, you will need black out curtains, and probably will have to call it an early night; lights attract attention, it *can not* look like there is anyone inside that van! Oh, and no running the heater or air conditioner, those make noise!

Or maybe you have been watching the adventures of an environmentally conscious young fellow, driving his Class B across the country, bugging out off grid to the wilderness, fishing for his dinner, cooking over a fire, nearly freezing to death as he camps out in the Alaska wilderness... really cool, really romantic, but that actually costs money. You will still need to pay for your car insurance, license, registration, gas, and, believe it or not, your chances of actually "bugging out and living off the land" 100% are not that good, so you will at least sometimes have to buy food. How will you support yourself, if you are "off grid"?

Maybe you saw some guy on You Tube, who scored a mold covered, 35' Class A from the 80's with a badly leaking roof and a bad case of mildew, for $500. He's planning on living for free, in the Walmart parking lot. Wow! $500! You think you can score something like that too! You could rebuild it, refurbish it, make it really cool with solar panels, and wind power, and a satellite system... OK, maybe. But really, do you have the construction and mechanical skills to do this? Do you know how hard it is to get rid of mold? Do you realize how expensive tires for an RV cost? Because the tires on your great Craigslist score are undoubtedly dry rotted. Do you have some place where it will be OK to leave this monstrosity all tore up, for months and months, while you fix it, without getting a ticket, or having the neighbors start a petition? If not, rescuing this wreck could cost you a a lot more than you anticipated! And "living for free, at Walmart" is simply not reality.

The same goes for building your dream RV from scratch, building a mobile tiny house, or turning a delivery truck into a stealth camper; all very do-able, but seriously consider your skills levels, your resources, your time, money, and if you have a space to do this, without running into trouble with the neighbors, building code enforcers or the police.

If your goal is to build something from scratch, you can find RV parts, like RV toilets and tanks, but also look into marine parts. Boats use many of the same sort of components, and some that are unique, and might be better suited for your plans. And don't forget, you will be moving, and your tiny house or homemade trailer will be under "earthquake conditions" going 60 mph down the highway! You need to teach yourself the techniques and principles of construction that will ensure durability and safety under these extreme conditions of shake, rattle and roll. A simple hammer and nails approach might lead to disaster. And design it as light as possible, excess weight can also lead to disaster.

Another thing, if you are building your own RV, a very important consideration is *weight distribution*; it is vital that the weight from side to side is even. For instance, it would be a very bad plan to put your tanks (water weighs 8 lbs per gallon) and your kitchen appliances all on one side, and just your bed on the other. If you want to build your own dream RV, please research the design aspect and the principle of weight distribution thoroughly.

I'm not trying to bash your dreams, just throwing in a reality check; you really need to think it out, and be honest with yourself, about your comfort and skill levels, practicality, and resources. Be prepared!

If your goal is to save money while going to school, or at your present low paying job, and you do not plan on traveling far, a travel trailer or $5^{th}$ wheel might fit the bill; you may be able to park it in the backyard of family or friends, or, put an ad on Craigslist for someone to rent you their backyard cheap, or in exchange for yard work or caretaking. Or you might get a night security gig. School or work in the day, keeping an eye on things at night. And if your living situation turns bad or evaporates, you can tow it out, and find a new place. "Stealth camping" on the streets might be do-able, but if you are going to school, you need to ask yourself, how this type of unstable lifestyle might affect your ability to study and get the good grades you really need. You might do just fine, but you might also find the underlying anxiety of sleeping on the street will start to affect your grades.

**Some deal killers (or serious re-negotiators) on purchasing an RV**

*Leaky roof, look for evidence of water spots on the ceiling, inside cabinets and closets*
*Moldy or mildew smell (indicates leaks)*
*Soft or spongy spots on the floor*
*Rust*
*It really looks like a trashed out junker*

If the RV you are looking at has been sitting for a long time, the tires are likely dry rotted (very dangerous, and expensive to replace) as well as any other rubber parts. Lubricants can be dried out, causing a potentially dangerous, or expensive, situation. If your RV has a surprisingly low mileage for it's age, it has been sitting in storage! Before you start driving it all over the place, take it immediately to a qualified mechanic, for a full inspection! You will SAVE money in the long run, if you can find the issues and fix them before they become expensive repairs!

So now, we come to the next part of this beginner's guide to an alternative RV lifestyle...

## Where to Park It?

Let's assume you have an interest in RV living as an alternative lifestyle, either because you can't afford to pay rent, are losing your home, or, you simply want more freedom to move and explore life. Maybe you have reasons, whatever reason, to want to get away from society and the general population. The first thing you need to do, after you figure out the type of lifestyle and RV best suited to you, is figure out where you are going to park it. *One important point: if you live somewhere with hot summers or very cold winters, "living for free" on the streets might not be realistic. You can not run an air conditioner without being hooked up to electricity (or running a noisy generator) and keeping warm enough in deep snow might be impossible.*

**First, let's discuss towables, fifth wheels and travel trailers.**
These are not suitable for urban stealth camping and blacktop boondocking. Sure, you can spend a night or two parking at Walmart, but unhitching it, and even putting out the slide outs (if you have them) will be frowned upon. You are going to have to find a safe place to park it, preferably with "full hook ups". (Hook ups are electricity, a water source, and a sewer to dump your waste water). This could be a trailer park, an RV resort, the backyard of a friend or family, or a night watchman job. If you are workamping, this will be provided for you. You might also place a classified ad, asking to rent someone's backyard (many homeowners are strapped for cash these days). But be aware, many towns and cities have ordinances against people living in trailers (or tiny houses) in backyards. Check your local codes. You might be OK, or you might find a work around; some places will allow a trailer for a "personal caretaker", someone caring for a sick, elderly or disabled person. You might be able to use that, if necessary. Or, maybe the location is obscure, hidden, and the neighbors don't care. You may also be able to find a property caretaking position. Another possibility is parking your trailer at a construction site, an RV or car dealership, or some other type of business with a big yard or parking lot, and doing "night security". If you live near a rural area with farms, you might be able to put up a classified for a work exchange or to rent a bare, solid, level patch of land on a farm.

Another option is renting at a trailer park; yes, it is rent money, but is often much cheaper than renting an apartment. If you need to go this route, factor what you may have financed on the trailer as part of the rent. Be prepared to be called (or to deal with) "Trailer Trash". Most places are decent enough, if all you could (not) afford before was low income housing, you will just be trading one type of low income neighbor for another. If things go downhill or get too creepy, you might be able to move away a little easier than renting an apartment.

If you can't find a place with "full hook ups", that's not totally unworkable; you can use an extension cord (heavy duty 12-14 gauge wire) to run into your landlord's house, dump your grey water into the bushes or on the lawn, and get a septic tank truck out to pump your black tank for you once every week or so. Or, if your landlord's house has a septic tank, you might be able to dump into that. Those septic tank pumping trucks are *very noisy,* and could easily generate complaints from the neighbors, and running your AC power off an extension cord can easily blow fuses, especially if you are running your air conditioner. You can run off your DC batteries, but keep in mind, air conditioners and microwaves are AC only, as well as the wall outlets, and unless you have enough solar panels to keep your batteries fully charged, you will have to plug in sometimes.

Another thing, make sure the ground where you plan to park your towable is solid and relatively level; if the yard is riddled with gopher holes, there will be a network of tunnels to cave in under you. Don't park it on sand. You can level the trailer with your leveling jacks, but only up to maybe a foot. Find the levelest and most solid and stable patch of ground available to you.

***Now, let's discuss motorhomes.*** You can find parking situations like those above for a trailer, plus a few more options. Many (but not all) Walmarts will allow you to stay in the back end of their parking lot for a night or two (or three, or four... don't push it!). You might map out all the Walmarts, and other big stores and shopping centers that allow overnight RV parking, and rotate them, moving to a different one each night, in order to avoid wearing out your welcome. *Indian casinos also often allow overnight RV parking, so if you have any casinos in your area, check it out. casinocamper.com and casinocampgrounds.com* You might also check into truck stops; it is generally OK to park amongst the big 18 wheelers for the night. Another place might be state route rest areas outside of town; check your state laws, not all states allow for overnight camping at rest areas. Also, be very careful; rest areas are notorious places for robberies and violent crimes, due to their isolation. (Although parking in the city is probably equally risky!)

Here are some businesses that may allow overnight parking. But check with individual stores; these days, with so many people looking to RVs as alternative housing, rather than as a "recreational vehicle" for vacationing, some stores are understandably revoking this courtesy, due to abuse by some mobile homeless. Remember, do not over stay your welcome, or abuse your privileges!

**Wal-Mart, Kmart, Target, Sam's Club, Costco, Meijer, Camping World, Cracker Barrel, Lowes, Menards, Flying J Truck Stop, Loves Travel Stop, Pacific Pride Fuel, Petro Truck Stop, Pilot Travel Center, TA Travel Center**

During the day, you can park in the back end of just about any big shopping center parking lot (be considerate, and do not block parking for their customers, or you may be asked to leave) the large parking lot of a city park (the police may stop by though, just to make sure you are not camping for the night), or many other places you might find. Just be aware of your size, and don't block the flow of traffic, or cause concern for the neighbors or passersby; stay low profile.

If you have one of the smallest Class Cs, a Class B or a truck camper, your options are even greater, due to your small size, and low profile look. You will be able to simply park on back streets, and lay low for the night. *But be very careful about where, and when, you choose to park!* You may find a safe, quiet suburban neighborhood.... the best plan of action may be, to come in after dark, after most working people are going to bed (let's say, between 9 pm and 11 pm) and park in an area that is not directly in front of anyone's house, like around a corner, alongside of a backyard fence, etc. You might try the back parking lot of a church, in a quiet, suburban neighborhood. Put up your blackout curtains, turn out the lights, and call it a night. When the sun starts to come up, start your engine, and pull quietly away, to your job, school, the parking lot of a shopping center, or someplace to get breakfast. Rotate your stealth camping areas! Do not become an unwelcome guest!

Another area that might be good for overnight parking is the local industrial area; you know, that part of town with all the auto mechanics, welding and machine shops and stuff, and no residential houses in sight. These areas are mostly abandoned after people get off work, except perhaps for handful of stray dogs, cats and homeless people. You might pull up shortly after sunset, and be able to stay into the morning, leaving as the workers arrive. Be careful here though, you may get a surprise visit from a crazy homeless person, or the cops, and these areas are isolated, leaving you prone to attack.

You may also find a hardly used dirt road going off into the brush, in a park, or out in the country, and park for the night. The idea is, to come and go in such a way that you do not attract attention. Of course, there is always "driveway camping" at friends and family. Once again, rotate these around, so as not to wear out your welcome, or attract unwanted attention from neighbors. You could also do house sitting, pet sitting, elderly person sitting.

*One important point, avoid schools! Trying to park your RV at an elementary school or high school at night may get you tagged as some sort of pervert, and colleges and universities can have pretty aggressive security!*

If you are a veteran, many outposts of the VFW (Veterans of Foreign Wars) will allow you to park overnight in the parking lot. *Also, there are military campgrounds available for active duty and retired military. militarycampgrounds.us and freecampgrounds.com/military.html*

Dumping and filling your tanks will also be simpler than with a towable, if you are living "homeless". Most RV parks will allow you to dump for a fee, usually $5-15. Some truck stops and gas stations also have dump sites, as well as state and county fair grounds, and some highway rest stops. A good plan may be to stay at a campground once a week or so, to dump and fill your tanks, and use their laundry and shower facilities. **One thing you may not know, many state and county fairgrounds also have RV spaces available, for a cheap price.** These were originally put in for events, such as the state fair, when exhibitors come and camp out for the duration. But regular people are also welcome to stay.

If you are living in your RV, especially a Class B or truck camper, but still have a fulltime regular job, getting a gym membership is a good idea; it will give you someplace to take a shower, get some excercise and hang out.

***A good, online resource for some free camping areas across the country is the "7 in 1 eBook" found on gypsyjournalrv.com*** You may have to hunt a little for the link, it keeps moving around, but *"The 7 in 1 eBook" covers Free Campgrounds, Fairground Camping, Casino Camping, RV Parks with Wifi, RV Dump Stations, RV "Good Guys", and the authors Favorite Restaurants.* It is not a 100% comprehensive list, but it is definitely a good place to start, and will give you some leads and clues.

Living for "free" in an RV on the streets is not an exact science; every town, city, RV and RVer are different. What is safe and OK in one place, could be illegal and dangerous somewhere else. Everyone needs to find their own comfort level and work out their own strategy, that is in tune with their environment.

***I am listing a few website resources here, between the in town and out of town camping, since these can go either way.***

**freecampgrounds.com**
**rv-camping.org**
**rvparkreviews.com**
**allstays.com/c/camping-free.htm** (look on the sidebar, Boondocking and Stops)

Membership site, Harvest Hosts, wineries and farms offering free overnight boondocking
**harvesthosts.com**

Membership site, network of other RVers hosting boondockers on their property
**boondockerswelcome.com**

There's more out there, these are just a few, so get online, and start searching "free camping", "boondocking" "blacktop boondocking", and "dry camping".

**For Those Taking the Journey Out of Town**

Maybe you want to make a run for it, and bug out from the big cities. You may have heard that you can ***camp for free on BLM land***. This is true, and not quite true... some BLM campgrounds do charge, but are much cheaper (and less developed, meaning no dump sites, electricity or water) than National Parks. They are also first come, first serve, do it yourself, no reservation affairs, unlike National Parks where reservations are required. You simply find a spot, and if it is a fee area, put some money in an envelope, and drop it in a box. Also, most of the BLM land is west of the Rockies, and away from the cities. You can check *BLM.gov*, or better yet, web search "blm camping" + your state, to get areas where you can camp.

There are some free and low cost camping options you may not have heard of, such as the ***Army Corps of Engineers.*** The Corps has had a hand in building many dams, and at the adjacent lakes, there are campgrounds. 422 lakes in 43 states, in fact. *Web search "Corps Lake Gateway".*
***corpslakes.usace.army.mil/visitors/camping.cfm***

Also, ***electric companies often have campgrounds*** at the lakes associated with their hydroelectric dams. For instance, *PG&E in California has nine campsite areas across the state.*
***pge.com/about/environment/pge/recreation*** Check your local utility companies to see if they offer recreation areas at their hydroelectric dams.

If you are a veteran, many outposts of the VFW (Veterans of Foreign Wars) will allow you to park overnight in the parking lot. *Also, there are military campgrounds available for active duty and retired military.* ***militarycampgrounds.us*** *and* ***freecampgrounds.com/military.html***

Of course, there are state and national parks, as well as county parks. These are fee site areas, and you generally need to make reservations, especially at the most popular ones. Generally, state and county parks operate on the "put some bills in an envelope, and drop it in a box" method, or may have a ranger station at the gate to collect fees. Check your local area for state and county parks. National parks, though, generally require a credit card, and a somewhat elaborate reservation making process, through *recreation.gov*

Another thing, many small towns across the West and mid-West offer free city park camping to RVers. These are the "near ghost towns", and they may offer free parking, just to attract a little business locally, such as when you gas up, or restock on groceries. Once again, *a good, online resource for some free camping areas across the country is the "7 in 1 eBook" found on gypsyjournalrv.com* You may have to hunt a little for the link, it keeps moving around, but *"The 7 in 1 eBook" covers Free Campgrounds, such as these small town parks.*

Another good resource is a membership to Passport America *passportamerica.com* For less than $50 a year, this will get you a card that will get you 50% off campground fees, and a big catalog of participating campgrounds across the country. It could pay for itself on just one stop!

## Basic Maintenance

I am certainly not a mechanic or a certified RV technician, but I can tell you a few of the basics on maintaining your RV. Walmart has most of the things you will need to maintain your RV, so while you are camping out in their parking lot, go inside, and stock up!

First, let's talk about appearance. You may say, looks aren't everything, my RV runs like a top! True, up to a point... if you want to successfully stealth camp or blacktop boondock, it is much better if you don't look like a bum. Sad, but true. There are upper and middle class people on vacation, then there are the mentally disabled, living in run down junkers. Which do you want to be perceived as? I can tell you what will give you a better reception, when you pull into the Walmart or Indian casino parking lot. That said, get yourself a long handled RV washing brush, and wash and wax the outside of your rig, just like you would a car (except there are special waxes, polishes and oxidation removers for the fiberglass siding common on RVs). If your decals (those silly stripes they paste all over) are peeling or really faded, you may consider removing or replacing them. Have pride in your ride, and keep your RV looking good! It will pay off in so many ways!

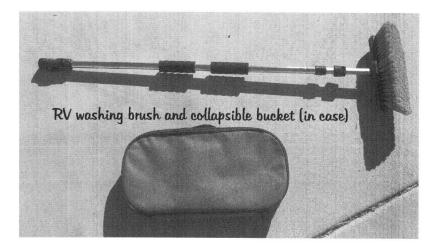

RV washing brush and collapsible bucket (in case)

Next, keeping the inside clean; I personally use as many organic cleaning products as possible. You are living in a small space, you don't need to be inhaling fumes. Also, when it comes to the RV plumbing system, harsh chemicals can damage things more easily than in a house. Be careful what you put down the drains! I simply clean out my sinks and toilet with dish soap. Just squirt some dish soap around the sink, and scrub it with a scrubby sponge or brush. If the sink or toilet get really stained, a little bleach is OK, rinse well!

Get a small "dust buster" type shop vac for the carpets. (This will only recharge on AC though). I clean the carpets (and upholstery) by spraying them with an organic citrus based stain remover, such as Bac Out, or Citrus Magic, and rubbing/wiping that down and into the carpet and upholstery with a rag. This also keeps things smelling fresh. (After living in your RV for a while though, you may come to the conclusion that carpet in an RV is a really dumb idea, and replace it with vinyl tile or wood).

Otherwise, keeping the inside of your RV clean is basically the same as a house or apartment. Just be mindful of avoiding harsh chemicals, both for your sake, and that of your RV.

## *The RV Plumbing System*

Once again, I am not a certified RV plumber, but I will tell you the basics. You need to get some RV toilet and black tank treatment; get the non-formaldehyde type. This stuff will help to break down the waste, and also keep the odor down. You can also pour a little of this into your sink and tub/shower drains overnight, to also help keep

those clear. Also, you can throw your pee pee toilet paper in the trash, rather than down the toilet, to lighten the solid waste load.

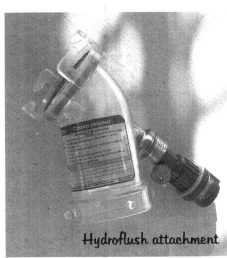

The size of your black tank, and how many people are using it, will determine how often you need to dump it. The average towable, Class A and Class C have 30 gallon black tanks (check how big yours is for sure) and can usually go a week to two weeks for one or two people. If you are a solo, figure on dumping every 10 days. *The usual procedure.... dump the black tank first, followed by the grey tank, to rinse out the hose.*

Look to see if your RV has a hose hook up on the outside to flush the black tank. If so, then your rig is equipped with a sprayer inside the tank, like a garden sprinkler, that will help to rinse out and flush any solid waste still int there. Always do this with the black tank valve open. If your RV does not have a built in flusher, you can get a spray wand to put down the toilet, and rinse it from the inside; but this is really only good if your pipe from the toilet drops straight down to the tank. If your pipes have some twists and turns, you can also get a "hydro-flush" attachment, which will back shoot water up into the black tank, and flush out any remaining solid waste.

Grey tanks are usually the same size as the black tank, but often have to be dumped more often, as dish washing and showers fill it up faster. Grey tanks should be dumped into a dump station, but in a pinch, could be dumped into the bushes, on a lawn, down a storm drain. But never, ever, ever dump your black tank anywhere but a dump station, or possibly down a septic tank.

Your rig will have a control panel, with lights displaying your different tank levels; fresh, grey and black. Check those to see where you are on levels. But be warned, the sensors in those tanks get clogged, and if your RV is old, they probably are. You can buy sensor cleaning treatments to put down your tanks, and one old trick for the black tank is, to dump a bottle of dishwasher soap and a bag of ice down the toilet before you start driving; the ice will swish the soap around and knock off any crud. If it seems as if your sensors are permanently stuck, just keep track of how often you dump.

Some things you will need for your sewer system besides the tank treatments, are a flexible sewer hose, and the fittings. Inspect your hose every so often; the metal coils can break inside, and even a tiny pinhole will rupture when you dump your tanks (a disaster if the hose breaks with the black tank dump!) It is a very prudent idea to keep an extra hose on hand, just in case your primary hose develops a leak.

When it comes to the fittings, you will need the bayonette attachments for the RV end, and an elbow pipe to fit into your sewer. Also, you will be paying it forward in convenience if you spend a little extra for the fittings. The E-Z Hose brand (the red fittings, that look like screws) will make getting the fittings onto a new hose a snap, you just screw the threads into the hose. The Blue-Line brand has slide on and off fittings that make attaching and removing the hose from your elbow easy. The cheaper types of fittings can be tough to get onto the hose; you may have to patiently warm the hose with a blow dryer, and gently stretch it until it will fit over the fittings. If you are boondocking, and don't have the AC power to run a blow dryer, you can lay the hose out in the sun, until it warms up enough to stretch. But if it is cold out, well, you will probably wish you spent a little

Presto-Fit BlueLine fittings make attaching to the elbow easy

more for an E-Z brand fitting that woud just screw in! Once you get your fittings on, secure them with a hose clamp.

*Fresh Water*

Attach the water regulator to the faucet, then attach a drinking water safe hose to it.

The first things you will need to get for the fresh water system is a water regulator, and a drinking water safe hose. The RV water system is made out of plastic tubing, not pipes, and can not take extreme water pressure. A water regulator will keep the water pressure coming into your RV at an acceptable limit. Place the water regulator onto the faucet, then place the hose onto the regulator. An ordinary garden hose may have chemicals leaching out into the water, so get a drinking water safe hose; these are usually white. And save yourself some headaches, and spend a little extra to get a "kink free" hose. You will need to roll the hose up and store it when moving, and the cheap hoses can kink up easily, creating frustrating blockages to the flow of water into the RV.

Water Filter

45

Another thing you might want to get for your fresh water is an inline water filter that attaches to the hose; these are relatively inexpensive charcoal based filters, that will help to purify your incoming water.

*Water Conservation*

If you are "dry camping" or "boondocking", one of the #1 issues is water conservation. You do not know how much water you are really using, until you live in an RV with a limited supply. A shower typically takes 5-6 gallons, as can washing the dishes. Doing dishes, taking showers, and all like that, as if you were still living in a regular house or apartment, could empty your tank in just 2-3 days for one person. You can find some creative solutions for conserving and recycling water, such as, saving dishwater in a large pot, and using it to flush the toilet. When running up the hot water, catch it while it's cold in a pitcher, turn off the water while shampooing or soaping up, and just turning it back on to rinse off. Only showering quickly once or twice a week, and taking "sponge baths" the rest of the week. You can use paper plates. There are a lot of ways to conserve water, so watch how you are using this most precious resource, and start thinking of ways to conserve!

Surge protector between the power source and the cord.

*The RV Electrical System*

The RV electrical system is really two electrical systems; an AC system, and a DC system. AC is "alternating current", and it is what you have in a regular house. DC is "direct current", and that is what you have in your car. These systems are separate in your RV. The overhead lights, the water pump, and the heater will run off your DC system, and the batteries in your RV. The wall outlets, the air conditioner, and the microwave are AC only, and will not work unless you are plugged into "shore power", meaning, plugged into an outside electrical outlet. There will be separate fuses for each; the DC fuses will be car fuses. See what type/size of fuses your RV has, and keep a few extra handy. Your RV will also have "cigarette lighter plugs" that go to the DC (battery) system. You can use these to power up your laptop and other appliances through the use of a *power inverter*. You can get power inverters at auto supply stores, and also online. Don't try to plug more than a 400 watt inverter into your cigarette lighter plug, it was not designed for that. If you need a more powerful inverter, then you can attach it directly to the battery.

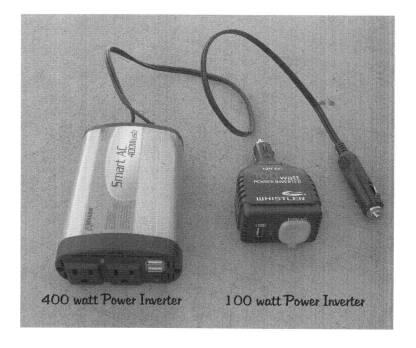

400 watt Power Inverter    100 watt Power Inverter

**Some typical *estimated* electrical useage of common appliances is:**

Blender/food processor: 300-400 watts
portable vacuum cleaner: 500-600 watts
mini-fridge: 600 watts
video game system: 20-30 watts
13" color TV: 80 watts
19" color TV: 160 watts
25" color TV: 225 watts
stereo amplifier: 240 watts
laptop computer: 100 watts
inkjet printer: 40 watts
fax machine: 120 watts
14" color computer monitor: 125 watts
electric heaters and blow dryers: 1,000 watts

The standard overhead lights in an RV are typically 12 watt car headlight bulbs; using your overhead lights carelessly can also drain your batteries. Replacing your incandescent bulbs with LED lights can save a lot of energy, typically, LEDs use 1/5 to 1/10 of the energy. (Keep in mind, LED bulbs can be *very* expensive! You can start by just replacing the lights you use the most). You can also supplement your lighting with solar powered lanterns, which you can leave on your dashboard to charge during the day. You can also get small solar chargers for cellphones and small electronics, which you can also leave on the dashboard.

As you can see, if you are boondocking and on DC power only, there are some appliances you will simply not be able to use, and even using lights at night can kill your batteries. *You must conserve your battery power! Unless you have solar panels or a gas or diesel generator, you batteries will drain, until you plug back into shore power to recharge them.* Even if you have solar panels, if you exceed the rate of recharge, your batteries will drain. So, you must conserve your battery power, in the same way you conserve water.

### *Solar Panels*

Solar panels are relatively affordable; you can have a basic 120 watt solar panel and a regulator to keep your batteries charged, professionally installed for typically $500-$800. If you can do it yourself, it will cost less. If you are doing it yourself, typically, the wires are fed through the refrigerator vent, and then to the electrical system and battery. A solar panel is an investment you will not regret!

## *Your RV Kitchen Appliances*

Your stove and oven will run on propane. Keep a long BBQ lighter to light them. It is safer, and more conservative propane use, to not leave your oven pilot light on. You RV refrigerator will either be a "two way" or "three way" refrigerator. The full size refrigerators are typically two ways. That means they can run on either AC electric, or propane. The smaller refrigerators common to Class Bs and truck campers can be three ways; AC, DC and propane. There will be a switch on the refrigerator to switch it to the different modes, as well as an "auto" switch, to automatically switch it when you unplug the RV from shore power. Your water heater will typically be either propane, and/or AC/propane. Typically, you will need to switch it to propane yourself, and the switch will be on your control panel.

## *If You Have a Built in Generator*

If you have a motorhome with a built in generator, this will also recharge your batteries when you run it. It's advised to run your generator once a month or so, just to keep it in shape. Also, this is a small engine, and needs to have oil changes, as well as filter changes. Look up the model of your generator, and find out how often to do this, as well as the type of oil it needs. Also, you may need to plug in your shore power cord into the generator, for it to power your AC system; look inside the compartment where your power cord is stored, and see if it has an outlet for the power cord.

*Winterizing*

If you live in a cold climate, where it freezes and snows, you will have to take precautions with your RV during the winter. Freezing water and sewer lines can burst, and the term "winterizing your RV" means draining all the lines, and/or filling them with a special RV anti-freeze just for this purpose. Of course, if you are living in it, this would not be practical. You can also make sure the RV is well insulated, buy a heated water hose, which you can plug in, and other techniques to ensure your hoses don't freeze and burst. Or, you can also drive south for the winter!

*For a more complete overview and repair manual for your RV systems, get a copy of **Woodall's RV Owner's Handbook**. You can find this on Amazon, and some RV supply stores.*

## Weight Distribution

It is very important not to overload your RV. When you are living in it fulltime, you need what you need to live a relatively normal lifestyle, but you also need to keep your possessions and tools streamlined. Just as you need to be conservative with your water and electrical use, you need to also to be conservative with your personal belongings. Get rid of anything you haven't used or worn in a long time. Streamline your books, keeping only the ones you really need. Keep only the pots and pans you use all the time, get rid of the rest. Some people will put things into storage, and pay storage fees every month, for stuff they never actually use. Many RVers who have paid for storage, month after month, eventually just get rid of that stuff anyways.

*Before you move into your RV, have a big yard sale, or go to the flea market, and get rid of anything you don't really need! Then, get rid of even more stuff by donating it to charity. Get it down to what you can really use, and really fit, into your RV.*

You also need to be aware of how you are distributing your weight; that means, don't load up one side of your RV with all the heavy stuff, making the load lopsided going down the highway. This can be very dangerous. If you have decided to build your own RV, such as a bus or delivery truck conversion, a tiny house, or a do-it-yourself trailer, you need to plan out your weight distribution. This is something you may want to get a professional opinion on.

Look around your RV for a sticker, usually a full page size, often in the clothes closet. This sticker will have all of your RVs weight capacities. Take this stuff seriously! Do not overload your rig! *Here is an example of the weight sticker inside of a clothing closet:*

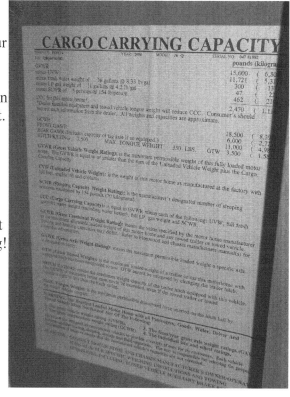

There will be other stickers around your RV, with more valuable information. Locate them.

51

Here is a sticker near the driver's seat, with more weight information, as well as the tire pressure information; note, the front and rear tires on this RV require different pressure, 80 psi in the front, and 90 psi in the back. This is common. Find out what your tire pressure should be for front and back, and maintain it! Over or under inflated tires can be very dangerous when carrying this much weight.

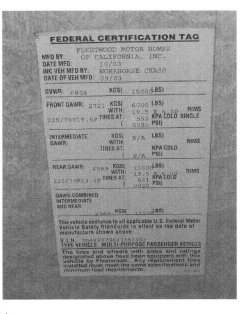

Here is a sticker located in a key cabinet over the door. It repeats some of the information, plus some.

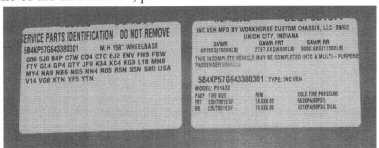

*A luggage rack like this, inserted into the hitch reciever is an example of tongue weight*

## Packing Your Stuff for Moving

Obviously, you need to secure your stuff inside the RV so it doesn't fall down while you are driving around. A motorhome will have a smoother ride than a towable, so stuff will stay in place a little better, but you still need to secure everything.

You can secure wall pictures and table top nic-nacks with Museum Putty. This is a white, plasticky putty, which will not stick to your fingers, but will stick things down to a table or wall. It is easily removable, and will not leave a residue. Museums and art galleries use it to secure valuable statues and artifacts from being knocked over. It is commonly available in California with the earthquake supplies, but in other states, you may need to look around, go to an RV store, or buy it online.

One cheap solution to a lot of packing is rubber shelf liner; you can often find this at the Dollar Store. Get a few rolls, and line every shelf. You can also cut strips of it to lay between your ceramic and porcelain dishes, make a sleeve for your coffee and tea pots, and lots of other uses.

Rubber shelf liner, also strips between the dishes, and wrapped around the French Press coffee pot. Dish towels wrapped around the coffee cups.

Another solution for packing things securely, is using nets and curtain rods inside the cabinets. The small, spring loaded curtain rods can be used to block things from falling out, and you can get some inexpensive net laundry bags, and cut them to fit your cabinets, and secure them with velcro (you may want to also put a staple into the velcro, for extra security when pulling the net off). You can also use small zip ties to secure a piece of net to some curtain rods to hold stuff back from falling out of an overhead cabinet.

Nets zip tied onto curtain rods

Nets with Velcro holding back some books which slid loose during travel.

*Curtain rods in the bathroom cabinet*

## Personal Safety

Personal safety is important, and if you are living a mobile lifestyle, it may seem even more important; but I'm not sure being on the road is all that much more dangerous than living in an apartment or a house. If you are a woman living alone, and you have a local neighborhood pervert, he already has been watching you, knows your schedule... and you may be a sitting duck. Moving around keeps certain people from focusing on you, and getting ideas. On the other hand, in certain places and situations, you may seem like a duck out of water, and an easy target.

One rule of thumb is, safety in numbers; if you see other RVers parked somewhere, you might want to park there too... unless they are the unsavory variety of "mobile homeless". But parking alongside the other travelers in the Walmart or Casino parking lot is rarely a dangerous move.

RV resorts and campgrounds are also probably safer than an average neighborhood; most of the other RVers are either retirees, or middle class families on a vacation. Financially secure old people, and middle class families on vacation, are pretty safe demographics.

Where you may run into trouble is if you are urban stealth camping; drug addicts, gangs and the mentally ill can be aggressive, and the police and home owners may object to you sleeping in your vehicle. All I can say about safety is the obvious; steer away from the inner city, and into a quiet, suburban neighborhood, keep your doors locked, keep a low profile, and be ready to start the engine and take off.

Having a dog is a good move; most campgrounds accept dogs, and a barking dog can be a deterrent; one note, a "little yapper" may fit into your RV nicely, but won't scare anyone. On the other hand, Pit Bulls and Rottweilers may be prohibited in certain campgrounds and even in certain cities. If you don't already have a four legged friend, but are considering a dog for companionship and protection, it may be prudent to get a dog that has a "big dog bark" and enough size and the looks to back up the threat.

You may be thinking about carrying a gun, a stun gun, or pepper spray. Those are not bad ideas, but be aware, each state and local government has different laws concerning each. A stun gun may be OK in one place, but not another. You may have a concealed carry permit in your home state, but that does not grant you the legality to carry concealed everywhere you may go. If you are carrying weapons, know how to handle them safely, and know the laws in each state you pass through, to cover yourself legally.

Personal safety on the road is mostly common sense, and situational awareness; *stop day dreaming, get out of your own head, and look around!* Is there anyone watching you? Any cars slowing down to take a look? Are there security cameras? Are there apartments or houses around, which might have an observer? If you have to leave, what is the best escape route? *Don't just look around, also listen up!* As you are going about your business in your RV, also be aware of any unusual sounds out there (this is where a dog comes in real handy!) If someone comes up to your door, you don't have to open it, just speak to them through a window. Keeping a barrier, or a distance, at least an arms length, between you and a stranger is never a bad idea.

## Where Are You From?

This is generally just a simple conversation starter, and as a fulltime RVer, that may be a tough question to answer.... and you may want to be careful how you answer that. Believe it or not, there could be legal ramifications if you answer that wrong. Do you have children? Are they being home schooled by you, in the RV? Well, in some states, home schooling is illegal, and I have heard stories of fulltime RVers losing (temporarily) custody of their children, because the kids answered the question, "Why aren't you in school?" wrong. Also, if you are parked in some states for a certain amount of time, and are making money in that state, they will want to collect state income tax from you. So the question, where are you from, and what do you do for a living, has cost a few fulltimers financially, when they said the wrong thing to the wrong person. And once again, laws and attitudes concerning weapons are different in each state, and letting on that you are carrying a concealed weapon in the wrong place, could land you in jail on a weapons charge. *Play it and say it safe; when you are outside your home state, just say, "I'm on vacation"!*

## Driving, and Planning Your Routes

*One thing to note related to driving, routes and safety; your usual AAA you had for your car won't cover an RV. You can upgrade your AAA membership to include road side assistance for an RV, or go with an RV specific company. Also, you RV insurance may have road side assistance.*

If you are venturing across the country, there are a few resources you should have, to help you plan your routes. The Mountain Directory ***mountaindirectory.com*** is indispensable in helping you to drive around the steep grades. Yes, winding mountain roads can be very scenic and fun to drive in a sports car, but they can be dangerous with an RV, and very hard on your brakes, transmission and engine. It may be best to plan your trips around such roads. *Take the truck routes.* If you do find yourself coming down a steep grade, *don't ride the brakes.* Your RV is not a car! It's best to hit the brakes hard, in short bursts, when you need to slow it down. Also, you can slow down with the engine, by shifting down into a lower gear. Using the lower gears may also be best when going up a hill.

Get a big map book of the United States, as well as local maps; many campgrounds have them for free. You may also want to ask other RVers at the campground what the best routes are; others who have come from the direction you are going can have invaluable information. And of course, you can get a GPS unit, and phone apps to help you find your way.

And don't forget to check the weather! You may be in warm and sunny Arizona in March, and think, Montana sounds like fun... only to find yourself stuck in a snow storm. You should also look up the weather history of a place, to see what the weather is typically like at the times you want to go. Once again, an RV is not a car, and it would be wise and prudent to avoid driving in snow or other extreme weather conditions!

One thing you will experience in an RV you may not have experienced in a car are high winds, and "blow back" from passing trucks. An RV is a "high profile" vehicle, and cross winds hitting your sides can literally blow your RV off course. Same with big rig trucks blowing past you. All you can do is hang on, and keep your eyes on the road for a white knuckle ride. If your rig gets seriously hit by high winds and trucks, or you live in an area with a lot of high winds, you might consider adding Air Tabs *airtabs.com* These are stick on "vortex generators" that artificially streamline your RV. The company claims they can save fuel, which most RVers haven't experienced, but they can help with vehicle handling in high winds.

Know how high your rig is, and pay attention to overhead clearings! You don't have to worry about gas stations or tunnels with a car, but you do with an RV, especially the really tall 5$^{th}$ wheels. If you have a really tall RV, you might want to check out the clearances of any tunnels and bridges on your routes.

Unless your RV was specifically built to go off road, *don't go off road!* Or at least, not too far off road! Class As and Class Cs, and even most of the lighter, van-like Class Bs, as well as towables, should only be driven on paved roads, or very good dirt roads. Ruts, trenches, and sand could leave you stranded, waiting for a heavy duty tow truck to rescue you (that is, if you can get a cellphone signal). Bad roads can also do damage to your RV. Be careful of where you pull over on the road; you may be able to pull a car off on a narrow or soft road shoulder, but don't try it with an RV. Keep your rig on solid ground!

## Towing

If you have a travel trailer, get a "weight distribution hitch", for safer and more stable driving and handling. You can also get hitch locks, to both secure your hitch (which is expensive) to your truck, and another one to prevent anyone from hitching up your trailer, and stealing it. Get the dealer who sells you the hitch how to use it, and practice.

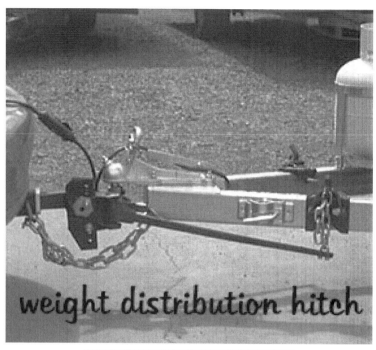

weight distribution hitch

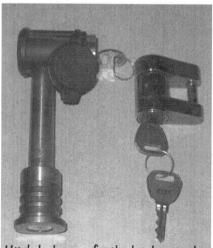

Hitch locks, one for the hitch onto the truck, and one to lock the trailer, to keep it from being stolen

## Off Into the Sunset...

Many people have said, "I'll just live in an RV for a few months, until I can get things together..." and they never go back. For them, life living light on the road is surprisingly easy and satisfying. If you are well prepared, not only physically and financially, but also mentally and emotionally, you may not go back either.

Living fulltime in an RV may bring you closer to your family, allowing you to travel and visit more often, or it may finally cut the ties. Your sense of "place" will be upended; you may find being cut loose from "place" the ultimate liberation, or the ultimate anxiety. You may be spending quite a bit of time alone, and your lifestyle will put you outside the norm of society. That may cause you to feel lonely, or liberated. You need to think about it, feel about it, and experience it for yourself.

I hope this book has at least given you a clue as to what to expect, and wish you the best on your journey!

Made in the USA
San Bernardino, CA
11 December 2014